WILDERNESS
ADVENTURES

# Hiking

Seth Kingston

**PowerKiDS**
press

NEW YORK

Published in 2022 by The Rosen Publishing Group, Inc.
29 East 21st Street, New York, NY 10010

First Edition

Portions of this work were originally authored by Suzanne Slade and published as *Let's Go Hiking*. All new material in this edition was authored by Seth Kingston.

Editor: Caitie McAneney
Book Design: Michael Flynn

Photo Credits: Cover (hiker), p. 5 franckreporter/E+/Getty Images; cover, pp. 17, 19, 23, 29 (mountain logo) doyz86/Shutterstock.com; interior (mountain background) Lidiia/Shutterstock.com; p. 5 Popartic/iStock/Getty Images; p. 7 Soft_Light/iStock/Getty Images; p. 8 ciud/iStock/Getty Images; p. 9 Peathegee Inc/Getty Images; p. 10 PATSTOCK/Moment/Getty Images; p. 11 miodrag ignjatovic/E+/Getty Images; p. 12 Petri Oeschger/Moment/Getty Images; p. 13 blazekg/iStock/Getty Images; p. 14 homeworks255/iStock/Getty Images; p. 15 dmbaker/iStock/Getty Images; p. 17 Halfpoint/Shutterstock.com; p. 19 RuslanDashinsky/iStock/Getty Images; p. 20 eclipse_images/E+/Getty Images; p. 21 Eureka_89/iStock/Getty Images; p. 23 David Trood/DigitalVision/Getty Images; p. 24 kellyvandellen/iStock/Getty Images; p. 25 noblige/iStock/Getty Images; p. 26 Ed Reschke/Stone/Getty Images; p. 27 Kresopix/iStock/Getty Images; p. 28 Jordan Siemens/Stone/Getty Images.

Library of Congress Cataloging-in-Publication Data

Names: Kingston, Seth, author.
Title: Hiking / Seth Kingston.
Description: New York : PowerKids Press, 2022. | Series: Wilderness
    adventures | Includes index.
Identifiers: LCCN 2020039434 | ISBN 9781725329355 (library binding) | ISBN
    9781725329331 (paperback) | ISBN 9781725329348  (6 pack)
Subjects: LCSH: Hiking--Juvenile literature.
Classification: LCC GV199.52 .K46 2022 | DDC 796.51--dc23
LC record available at https://lccn.loc.gov/2020039434

Manufactured in the United States of America

Some of the images in this book illustrate individuals who are models. The depictions do not imply actual situations or events.

**Note to Parents and Teachers:** Some of the activities in this book require adult supervision. Please talk with your child or student before allowing them to proceed with any wilderness activities.

CPSIA Compliance Information: Batch #CWPK22. For further information contact Rosen Publishing, New York, New York at 1-800-237-9932.

Find us on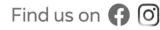

# CONTENTS

# Take a Hike!

Hiking can take you across some pretty amazing **terrain**. People hike up mountains, along rivers, and even across countries. Some hikes take only an hour or two, and loop around to where you started. Others take weeks or even months, and can take you somewhere you've never been before.

Many people hike because it helps them relax and exercise. Hiking allows you to spend time in the fresh air and in the company of good friends. People enjoy hiking because they often discover new things in nature. They can encounter animals in their natural environments, like foxes and black bears. They spend time among different plant life, like redwoods or cacti. Some climb mountain peaks to enjoy the view at the top. Hiking can take you anywhere!

Hiking is great exercise. It's good for building strength, gaining **endurance**, and helping you feel calmer and happier.

# Where Can You Hike?

You can find hiking trails anywhere you live or travel. Even cities can have trails nearby. It's important to plan ahead and research the trails in your area, or wherever you're traveling. Some websites have reviews of trails and rate them from easy to expert. It's important to keep in mind the distance, fitness level, the time of year and weather, and **elevation** gain. The more the elevation gain, the harder the hike!

You can often find both easy and challenging trails in state and national parks. Park trails often have signs that help keep you from getting lost, and maps that tell you how long or difficult a trail is. Hiking can help you connect with your hometown or a travel destination in a new way.

# WILD FILE

If you're hiking while on a trip, you can talk to locals about the trails in the area. Word of mouth and guidebooks are great resources for choosing your hike.

Some people travel around the world to take a hike, exploring jungles, mountains, and coastlines.

# Be Prepared

As with any wilderness adventure, you have to be prepared for any possible challenge. The gear you pack will depend on the time of year and weather. You might need snowshoes in the winter, or lots of sunscreen and a hat in the summer. No matter the weather, you need a good pair of hiking shoes or boots. Boots provide support and protection for your feet. Make sure to choose a pair that fit well, have good **traction**, aren't too heavy, and are waterproof.

Some people use trekking poles or a hiking staff on steep or long trails for extra support and balance.

Important hiking gear includes a **GPS** or compass, headlamp, sun glasses and sunscreen, a first aid kit, matches or a lighter, and a multi-tool like a Swiss army knife. For more extreme hikes, pack a bivvy—an emergency sleeping bag. Always pack extra clothes, food, and water.

# Follow That Trail!

Once your hiking bag is packed and your boots are laced tight, it's time to hit the trail. It's often good to start a trail earlier in the day, especially in warmer months. The more daylight you have, the better.

Beginning hikers should follow marked trails. Marked trails have signs along the way so you will not get lost. Most parks provide maps of their marked trails. On the map, you'll see the length and difficulty of each trail. Trails are usually labeled easy, moderate, hard, or very hard. Easy trails are generally short. They will take you over flat land or small hills. Hard trails are longer and may include rough, steep areas. It's smart to start with an easy trail when you're new to hiking!

Who are you hiking with? Pick a trail that everyone in your group can complete.

# Types of Trails

Your trail will start at a trailhead. Many trailheads have markers with the name of the trail. Some have maps and information about the hike. Some have a sign-in book to track the people who use the trail.

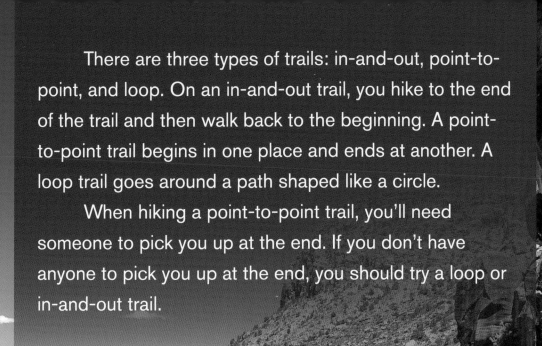

There are three types of trails: in-and-out, point-to-point, and loop. On an in-and-out trail, you hike to the end of the trail and then walk back to the beginning. A point-to-point trail begins in one place and ends at another. A loop trail goes around a path shaped like a circle.

When hiking a point-to-point trail, you'll need someone to pick you up at the end. If you don't have anyone to pick you up at the end, you should try a loop or in-and-out trail.

You can find many types of trails in some of the world's most stunning locations, like the Grand Canyon.

# A Day in the Woods

Day hikes are often for people with any fitness level or hiking experience. Day hiking doesn't require a lot of extra gear. When choosing a trail for a day hike, you need to make sure you have enough hours of sunlight in which to complete it. It's a good idea to tell others about your hiking route and when you plan to return.

If you're going to hike for more than a few hours, you might bring a small backpack along, called a day pack. Depending on the length of your hike, you may need sunscreen, a first aid kit, bug spray, food, and water. It's always smart to carry an extra layer of clothes or dry socks, just in case.

MOSQUITO REPELLENT SPRAY
PLEASANT SCENT, DEET FREE, CHILD SAFE

NO MORE BITES

EFFECTIVE NATURAL REPELLENT
REPELS MOSQUITOS, FLIES, FLEAS AND TICKS

SPRAY LOTION

CAUTION   KEEP OUT OF REACH OF CHILDREN

Hiking takes a lot of energy, even when it's only a day hike. Make sure to pack food and water, especially in the summertime.

# Overnight Trips

Overnight trips require a bit more planning, packing, and preparation. They're often best suited for people with hiking and camping experience who can complete more difficult trails. When you take an overnight hiking trip, it's called backpacking. This kind of hiking takes endurance and wilderness skills, like pitching a tent or setting up a **hammock** for sleep.

Backpacking requires more gear than day trips. Backpackers bring a tent, sleeping bag, flashlight, matches, food, and water. Some bring a small stove for cooking. When hiking overnight, plan ahead so you will know where you can set up your tent or hammock. Also, plan what you'll eat and how you'll prepare the food.

## WILD FILE

Many backpackers carry either a **hydration** pack or a water filter. Hydration packs often include a **reservoir** and drink tube.

# FOOD FOR THE TRAIL

You need enough food to keep your energy up when you're backpacking. However, there are several challenges to bringing and preparing food on the trail. You'll need food that's lightweight and won't spoil, or go bad. Canned foods are heavy and fresh foods spoil. Many backpackers eat **dehydrated** foods, like beef jerky or dried fruit. You can buy freeze-dried meal pouches, packets of tuna, or calorie-dense bars. Keep your food in a container called a **bear cannister** to keep animals from taking it.

Make sure to practice pitching your tent before you leave for your overnight trip.

17

# What's the Weather?

Everyone likes hiking on a sunny, warm day. But people hike in all seasons and in all weather. Sometimes that means rain, snow, or extreme temperatures. It's important to always check a weather **forecast** before you leave, listen to any trail warnings, and be prepared for the worst weather.

Hikers in the spring and summer enjoy warm weather and lots of wildlife. Many people like to hike in the autumn so they can see the colorful trees. Winter snow and ice change trails into beautiful white wonderlands. Each kind of weather has its own challenges, from sunburns to frostbite. In rainy months, pack waterproof clothes and footwear. In winter months, pack many layers of clothes to keep you warm.

# BEWARE THE SPRUCE TRAP!

If you're hiking in northern regions in the winter, you might come across a major hiking challenge—the spruce trap. Spruce trees are common evergreen trees, with fanned branches that can hold a lot of snow. Sometimes deep snow hides in the space between buried branches, and this is called a spruce trap. A hiker can step onto the snow trap and sink down up to their neck. To avoid spruce traps, stay on marked trails and steer clear of spruce tree trunks.

## WILD FILE

Winter gear might include snowshoes or crampons—spikes for your hiking boots. These tools can help you walk on icy or snowy surfaces.

Hiking in snowy weather requires different gear than hiking in warm, sunny weather.

# Let's Go Orienteering!

Some hikers look for a new challenge—orienteering. When you go orienteering, you find your way in nature using a map and compass. Many hikers use orienteering skills to know where they are during a hike. An orienteer uses a special map called a topographic map. A topographic map shows the height of certain land features, such as hills, mountains, and valleys.

Some orienteers compete in orienteering contests. The first public orienteering contest was held in Norway in 1897. At these events, people race across a large course using only a map and compass for guidance. They have to find different spots called controls on the course. The racers visit each control in a certain order. Competiters use their skills to find the best route for completing the course.

Some orienteers use GPS technology to record their controls and map their routes. However, it's against the rules to use GPS to find your way during the course.

# WILD FILE

A compass uses magnetism to point toward north. This tool helps hikers know which direction they're moving.

# Climbing Mountains

There's no mountain in the world that's too high to hike with the right skills and gear. Hikers who enjoy extreme hiking and new challenges may try mountaineering. Mountaineers climb steep mountains for fun. The higher the peak, the more **hazardous** the climb and weather conditions. Mountaineers learn special skills that allow them to climb over rocks and ice.

Climbing steep mountain sides requires safety measures. Mountaineers hold ropes fastened to the ground for safety. On rocky terrain, climbers wear a **harness**, which is tied to a rope. They use special tools, such as an ice hammer and crampons, for climbing through snow and ice. Crampons help a climber dig into an icy slope. Mountaineering may be difficult, but hikers get their payoff at the top—an amazing view!

# CLIMBING EVEREST

Mount Everest is the tallest peak on Earth, and hundreds of people climb it each year. Part of the Himalayan mountain range, it stands on the border of Nepal and Tibet. Everest's summit, or top, is 29,035 feet (8,849.9 m)–so high that mountaineers have to bring oxygen tanks to breathe. Its higher elevations have ice, snow, high winds, and **avalanches**. Native Tibetan and Nepalese high-altitude mountain workers guide mountaineers and carry their supplies to the top. Many don't make it to the top, and some even die.

## WILD FILE

Some mountaineers attempt to climb the "Seven Summits"–the highest peaks on each continent. They include Kilimanjaro (Africa), Everest (Asia), Aconcagua (South America), Denali (North America), Vinson (Antarctica), Carstensz (Australasia), and Elbrus (Europe).

Climbing up steep mountains or glaciers covered in ice is no small feat! It takes years of training to be able to complete this difficult glacier hike.

# Long Trails

Some trails, called thru-hikes, take months to finish, and hikers need to have endurance to finish them. The Appalachian Trail is 2,190 miles (3,524.5 km) long. It stretches from Georgia to Maine and crosses through 14 different states and 8 national forests. Anyone can hike parts of the Appalachian Trail on shorter trips, but thru-hikers attempt to make it all the way through the trail. Only about one in four people complete the Appalachian Trail, and it takes between five to seven months of hiking.

Appalachian Trail

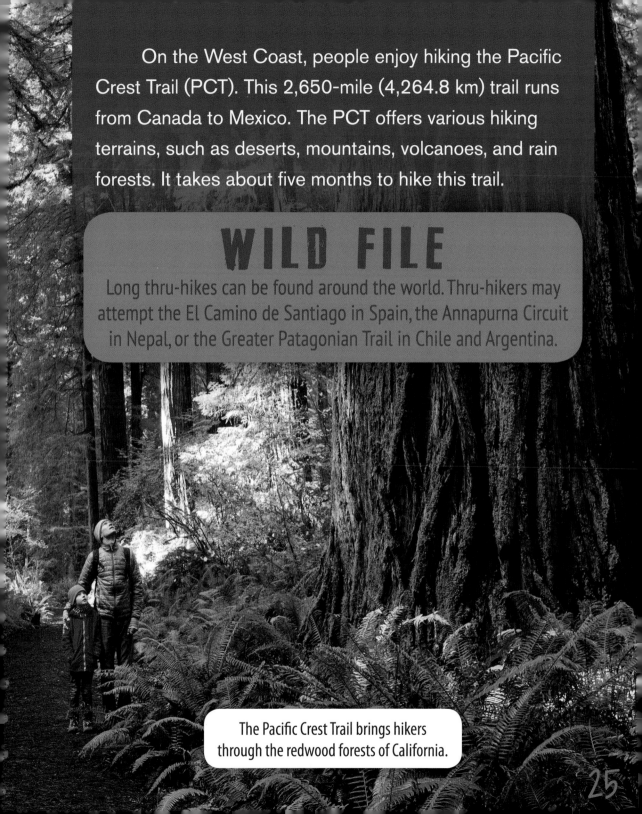

On the West Coast, people enjoy hiking the Pacific Crest Trail (PCT). This 2,650-mile (4,264.8 km) trail runs from Canada to Mexico. The PCT offers various hiking terrains, such as deserts, mountains, volcanoes, and rain forests. It takes about five months to hike this trail.

# WILD FILE

Long thru-hikes can be found around the world. Thru-hikers may attempt the El Camino de Santiago in Spain, the Annapurna Circuit in Nepal, or the Greater Patagonian Trail in Chile and Argentina.

The Pacific Crest Trail brings hikers through the redwood forests of California.

# Out in Nature

There's nothing like taking a hike out in nature.
You can observe wild animals, from tiny chipmunks
and salamanders to big black bears. You can watch
for birds perched in trees or deer running through
woods. Finding animals in nature can be exciting, but
it's important to stay a safe distance from them and
respect their space.

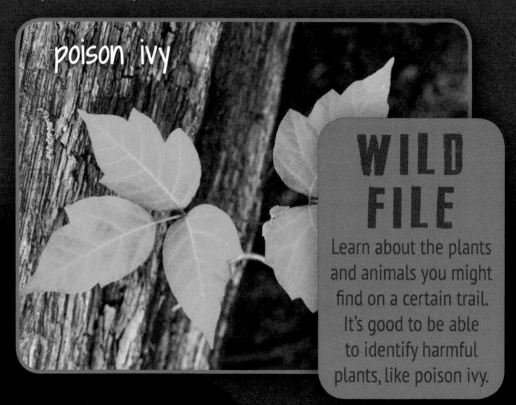

poison ivy

## WILD FILE

Learn about the plants
and animals you might
find on a certain trail.
It's good to be able
to identify harmful
plants, like poison ivy.

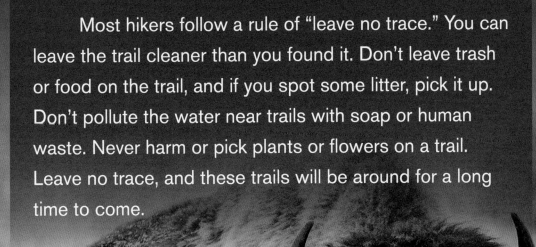

Most hikers follow a rule of "leave no trace." You can leave the trail cleaner than you found it. Don't leave trash or food on the trail, and if you spot some litter, pick it up. Don't pollute the water near trails with soap or human waste. Never harm or pick plants or flowers on a trail. Leave no trace, and these trails will be around for a long time to come.

bison

Different regions have different wild animals. Make sure to research the animals you may come across on your hike.

# Ready to Hike!

You've chosen your trail, packed your gear, and prepared for the weather. You're ready to hike! Remember safety in numbers, and always hike with an adult. You can even hike with a larger group of people. Hiking clubs exist in many regions that have trails.

Hiking is a great way to visit new places and try new things. On a snowy day, you could try hiking with snowshoes. On a clear night, you can use a headlamp to go for a night hike, observing animals that come out after dark. In the summertime, you can take a road trip to different trails around your state or around the country. There's always something new to discover when you're out on the trail.

> Snowshoeing can help you enjoy hiking trails even in the wintertime.

# SAFETY TIPS

► Never hike alone and always tell people where you're going.

► Make sure to pack and consume enough food and water as you hike.

► Steer clear of dangerous plants or plants that you can't identify.

► Look down as you hike—you don't want to trip over rocks or roots!

► Keep a safe distance from wild animals.

► Carry a first aid kit and emergency supplies when you go out hiking.

► Choose a trail that's a good fit for your skill level.

► Check a weather forecast before you leave for your hike. Never hike in a thunderstorm.

## WILD FILE

Hiking can allow you to set big goals and land big accomplishments, like hiking a high summit or a group of mountains. Some people, called 46ers, climb all 46 high peaks of the Adirondack Mountains.

# GLOSSARY

**avalanche:** A large mass of snow sliding down a mountain or over a cliff.

**bear canister:** A thick container that protects food from bears.

**elevation:** Height above sea level.

**endurance:** The power to do something hard for a long time.

**dehydrated:** Describing something from which water has been removed.

**forecast:** An informed guess about future weather.

**GPS:** Stands for Global Positioning System. A system that uses satellite signals to locate places on Earth.

**hammock:** A swinging bed made of cloth or netting.

**harness:** A set of straps that goes around someone's body.

**hazardous:** Involving risk.

**hydration:** Involving adding water to something.

**reservoir:** A place where something is stored.

**terrain:** The type of land in an area.

**traction:** The stickiness between two surfaces, such as a tire and a track.

# FOR MORE INFORMATION

## Books

Olsson, Helen. *Ranger Rick Kids' Guide to Hiking: All You Need to Know About Having Fun While Hiking.* Irvine, CA: Walter Foster, 2018.

Siber, Kate, and Chris Turnham. *National Parks of the U.S.A.* Minneapolis, MN: Wide Eyed Editions, 2018.

## Websites

### Discover the Trail
*www.pcta.org/discover-the-trail/*
Explore more about the Pacific Crest Trail, which stretches from Mexico to Canada.

### Hiking Facts for Kids
*kids.kiddle.co/Hiking*
Learn basic facts about hiking with this accessible resource.

**Publisher's note to educators and parents:** Our editors have carefully reviewed these websites to ensure that they are suitable for students. Many websites change frequently, however, and we cannot guarantee that a site's future contents will continue to meet our high standards of quality and educational value. Be advised that students should be closely supervised whenever they access the Internet.

# INDEX